HOW TO DEAL WITH NARCISSISTIC PEOPLE

How to Neutralize a Narcissist and Make Yourself Unattractive to Them

Table of Contents

Introduction

I want to thank you and congratulate you for purchasing the book, *"How to Deal with Narcissistic People: How to Neutralize a Narcissist and Make Yourself Unattractive to Them."*

This book has the power to help you live a better and happier life by providing you with actionable information and potent techniques to effectively deal with a narcissist.

If there is someone in your life who manipulates you by hurting you emotionally, physically and sexually, someone who ridicules you only to feel good about himself/ herself, and someone who is only outwardly pompous but has a tattered self-esteem from within, it is clear you are living with a narcissist. This feeling is definitely not pleasant because narcissists have the power to make your life a living hell.

The good news is that you can learn to neutralize their venom so that they stop treating you like a doormat and leave you alone. If you wish to have better control of your life and save yourself from the vicious control of a narcissist, this book is for you. It guides you on how to disarm a narcissist and appear unattractive to him/her so that you can move on with your life and live by your terms.

Thanks again for purchasing this book. I hope you enjoy it!

Chapter 1:
Understanding NPD and Its
Effects On Your Life

If you are in a frustrating, exhausting relationship with someone who always seeks constant admiration and attention from you, does not ever empathize with you or take your needs into consideration, thinks of himself/herself as the king of the world, and cannot handle even a hint of criticism, there is no doubt he/ she suffers from narcissistic personality disorder.

While narcissists certainly suffer from a serious disorder, the implications of their condition are faced by those around them. If you are living with someone who spews all his/her venom on you and manipulates you every step of the way only to feed his/her ego, it is time you learn more about narcissistic personality disorder and how living with that person is sabotaging you. This will motivate you to take the right measures to deal with them and live a much better life.

Narcissistic Personality Disorder (NPD)

The word narcissist is commonly used nowadays and often mistaken for someone who is self-obsessed, but in pure psychological terms, a narcissist is not just someone who loves himself herself unconditionally.

Narcissists suffer from NPD wherein they form a grandiose sense of self and fall in love with their inflated, idealized self because it helps them avoid feelings of incompetence and insecurity deep within. While narcissists pretend to be self-assured, calm and in control of their life, the truth is they are always freaking out from within and in search of someone to control and dominate.

NPD encompasses a pattern of arrogant and self-centered behavior and thinking along with a complete lack of compassion for people and an intense need of constant validation from others. Narcissists often come across as demanding, patronizing, selfish, cocky and manipulative. That said; their victims are often unable to identify such character traits and the distorted, selfish behavior at first because narcissists can be incredibly charming as well.

Narcissists are resistant to change their behavior even when they know they are the ones causing problems. They are extremely sensitive to their needs, but highly insensitive to those of others.

To feel good about themselves, they first charm people by being caring, sweet and loving towards them and through the power of manipulative language. Once the victim is drawn to them, narcissists begin their cycle of manipulation and control to attain a position of complete power over them.

Let us look at their character traits and how each one of those affects your life and wellbeing.

Have a Grandiose Sense of Self

Narcissists strongly believe they are superior to everyone else. Yes, they are mostly quite intelligent and even great at their work, but that does not give them a sense of entitlement over everyone else. Often, narcissists lie to prove themselves right as well as about their talents, accomplishments and potentials.

This means that if you are in a relationship with a narcissist, your conversation with the person will be limited to how amazing he/she is and how much he/she contributes to something, and how lucky you are to have him/her in your life. You won't ever get heard, feel loved and receive any appreciation from him/her unless he/she needs a favor from you.

Moreover, his/her grandiose sense of self may even compel him/her to ridicule you and negatively contrast you with himself/herself or others so he/she feels good about himself/herself. When this behavior continues for a long time, it takes a toll on your wellbeing because you become exhausted praising him/her, but not getting any attention yourself.

Are Defensive, Volatile and Overpowering

Reality does not always support the narcissist's grandiose sense of self. As much as he/she likes to believe he/she is the best at everything he/she does, he/she isn't always able to prove himself/herself.

Narcissists spin extreme self-glorifying tales of their brilliance, power and attractiveness to their victims and if the victims refuse to believe those, they get violent, defensive and extremely controlling. They can then go to any lengths to attain the admiration and submission they want including physical harm, sexual assault, emotional abuse and even gas lighting.

This means your abuser is likely to call you names, distort the truth to make you sound crazy, gaslight you, which means he/she questions your perception of reality and may even call you insane, hits and throws things at you, deprives you of attention, financial rights, love and sexual needs and ignores you completely, isolates you from loved ones, treats you nicely when he/she wants to, but bounces back to irrational behavior the minute you don't comply with his/her demands, blackmails you emotionally, invades your privacy, resorts to character assassination and can even cheat on you only to hurt you and compel you to serve his/her needs.

Exploits You without any Shame or Guilt

Narcissists do not have the ability to understand other people's feelings. They solely care about their own needs and wellbeing, and to fulfill that, they can go to any length to exploit their victims. Needless to say, they feel no shame or guilt in doing that because their sole purpose is to please themselves and nothing else.

If there is a narcissist in your life whether it is your neighbor, seemingly best friend, sibling, parent or your partner, it only means you will find yourself at their mercy and disposal every now and then to make them feel great about themselves and to make them feel entitled over you. This can happen every time he/she needs validation, but you are unavailable, every time you challenge their excellence and superiority, every time you do something for your own good and need, every time you ask them to fulfill your rights, every time you disagree with them; and every time you do not comply with their demands.

Life with a narcissist is definitely not easy because you lack complete control over it. As hard as it is to withstand a narcissist, the truth is you can effectively deal with him/her provided you use the right strategies. The following chapters will provide you with helpful and potent coping mechanisms to tame a narcissist so he/she stops treating you like their puppet.

Chapter 2:
See Them for Who They Are and
Set an Intention to Save Yourself

The major reason why you find it difficult to handle your narcissistic abuser is because you do not accept that he/she is a cold-hearted, manipulative controller who only knows how to please him or herself and does not care at all about you.

To seek his/her care, love and attention, you plead with him/her, retaliate if he/she does not listen to you, defend and explain yourself, argue and reason with him/her, threaten him/her and seek an understanding. All these behaviors won't ever yield you any positive results because you are dealing with a narcissist.

The very first step that you need to take towards your betterment is to see your abuser for who he/she really is, accept his/her true identity and set an intention to break free of their twisted, manipulative tricks.

See a Narcissist for Who He or She Really is

When the need arises, a narcissist can quickly turn on his/her charm and draw you towards his her grand promises, ideas and charisma. This is why you haven't been able to fully decipher his/her hidden agenda and understand the fact that you are dealing with a ruthless person. You allow him/her to overpower you because you do not see him/her for who he/she truly is.

Put an end to this malicious cycle by closely observing his/her behavior for some time. Watch how he/she treats people and look for the following signs:

- He/she always talks sweetly when he/she needs a favor from someone.
- He/she is exceptionally nice to certain people at certain times, but incredibly ruthless with others.
- He/she gets excited when his/her topic of interest comes up.
- He/she cannot stop talking about his/her potentials, talents and achievements and often tells bizarre, extraordinary stories of his/her victories that only seem too good to be true.
- He/she has severe anger management problems and his/her anger often triggers when someone fails to comply with his/her demands.
- He/she blames you or others for all their problems.
- He/she blatantly disrespects people and uses their weaknesses to strong arm them.
- He/she belittles people, makes fun of them, calls them names and humiliates them in front of others.
- He/she fails to take your needs into account and keeps ignoring you unless he/she is in need of your support.

- He/she has an explosive personality and once he/she gets triggered, he/she can make life chaotic for you and others.

If you spot any 2 to 3 of these behaviors, or all of them in someone close to you, it is clear he/she is a narcissist. You need to accept the fact that he/she has a serious personality disorder and stop denying it. Those living with narcissists often share a very close bond with them as narcissists manipulate them through the power of their word and keep telling them how they are special to them and that their relationship is extraordinary. This keeps the victims hooked to their abuser and prevents them from accepting their problem.

Once you see your abuser behaving this way, accept he/she has a serious problem and if he/she does not agree to work on himself and take the necessary steps to change, then you need to at least take care of yourself.

Become Motivated to Look After Yourself

Close your eyes for a few moments and think of how you are allowing your life to slip from underneath your hands by not taking care of yourself, doing things you want, pursuing your ambitions and living it on your terms. Think of all the times you wanted to make a different career choice, enroll in a cooking class, go on a holiday or do anything that brought you happiness, but sacrificed it because your controlling abuser wanted things differently.

Think of how you are wasting precious moments of your life living with that selfish, self-centered person or working for him/her in case he/she is your boss, and how you wished for things to be different. Write down everything that you wish to do and imagine yourself actually living that life. Involve yourself in the imagination by adding colors, details, expressions, sounds and sights to it so it feels real to you.

By now, you'll feel pumped enough to look after yourself and put an end to the narcissistic abuse you have been suffering from. At this point, write down your intention to do so and chant it out loudly, confidently and clearly. It could be anything such as, 'I am ready to take charge of my life and put an end to the narcissistic abuse I am suffering from.' Once you chant it about 10 times, change the intention to a suggestion that states how you are actually working towards living a better life such as 'I am looking after myself and focusing on my needs' to feel focused on yourself. Practice this suggestion daily and start shifting your attention from your abuser towards yourself to strip them off their power.

Now that you are all set to take care of yourself and stop being your abuser's prey, stop showering attention on to him/her all the time. The next chapter tells you how to do that.

Chapter 3:
Stop Giving Them Attention
and Focus on Yourself

With a narcissist in your life, it is likely that attention will gravitate his/her way. Be it positive or negative attention, a narcissist works hard to keep himself/herself in the spotlight. You may have found yourself buying his/her tactic, pushing aside all your needs only to satisfy your abuser. Whether he/she wants you to coddle him/her at 3am at night, or leave your work to run errands for them, or listen to their incessant stories of superficial valor and excellence, you are ever ready to tend to them to please them.

While you may have felt happy tending to their needs at all times, you do often think about how nice it would feel to look after your own needs. Now that you have set the intention to break free of their abusive claws, it is only right to stop showering unnecessary attention onto them. Here's how you can do that.

Do Not Focus on Him/ Her

Start looking out for your own needs and wellbeing by not focusing on him/her for once.

- Make a list of all your needs and wants that you have ignored for quite a long time and think of why you must meet those needs.

- Think of all the times when you wished your abuser to look after your wellbeing, but he/she did not.

- Set a time during the day to focus on your needs and prepare for it beforehand. For instance, if you have had a bad cough and a terrible backache for 2 weeks now, set a doctor's appointment for the next day at a convenient time. Similarly, if you have wanted to get a massage for months now, but could not due to one obligation or another (usually not yours), get an appointment for one now. Whatever your needs and tasks are, be it professional or personal, create a schedule for them. Once you do that, set reminders for it and chant suggestions based on them such as 'I am going to get a manicure on (date and time)' or 'Tomorrow, I will call a client' and so on. This feeds the suggestion in your subconscious mind and helps you focus on it.

- If you live with your narcissistic abuser, or if he/she has any involvement in your life, inform him/her of your unavailability at certain hours, but only if need be. For instance, if your abuser is your boss and your doctor's appointment is during work hours, you'll need to inform him/her beforehand.

- When it is time for you to attend to that task/appointment, simply leave for it or engage in the task/activity if you are supposed to do it from home.

- If your abuser sees you leaving and inquires about it, be upfront and firmly tell him/her that you are going to run a personal errand and leave. In case, he/she asks you not to go and issues an order, refuse point blank and tell him/her that you are running late. Make sure to quickly leave or else you may find yourself surrendering to his domination and charisma.

- Likewise, say no to him/her every time he/she needs you to do something, but you do not wish to engage in that task. It will take you time and practice, but soon you will get the hang of saying NO.

Saying no to him/her is hard and doing things you want is even harder particularly because you do not have the habit of doing so, but once you do take care of your needs and address important things in your life, you will realize how positively busy your life becomes leaving you with hardly any time to worry about the self-centered person.

Do Not Praise Him/ Her or Talk to Him/ Her Unless Necessary

Narcissists crave for attention and admiration at all times. If he/she feels down and upset, he/she is likely to come to you for approval and validation, and by now you must have built the habit of appreciating him/her and telling him/her how amazing he/she is even if you don't truly mean it. You need to stop doing that because even if your praises aren't genuine, they feed his/her ego and make him/her act like your God.

Every time your abuser insinuates he/she wants your approval and fishes for compliments, simply flash a nice smile at him/her, nod your head and continue to do what you were doing in the first place.

Do not make direct eye contact with him/her, and do not ask him/her questions about his/her feelings until and unless it is absolutely necessary.

Expect Things to be Different

When you start ignoring your abuser and shift attention from him onto yourself, he/she too may behave differently at first. Anticipate things to change in the start because you are changing too. He/she may ignore you, not speak to you, may act more aggressively, may even threaten to leave you and may give you complete silent treatment at all times.

Do not retaliate to any of such behaviors and accept them openly. Do not speak to him/her about his/her changed behavior and understand that it is a result of your changed behavior. He/she will do that only to get your attention and pick a fight with you, but you need to act strong. The more you ignore his/her new behavior, the more powerful you'll appear to him/her and the more you will defuse him/her.

Remind Yourself of Your Strengths

While you try to focus on your wellbeing, you may find yourself in situations where your abuser tries to upset, ridicule and demean you. He/she may also try to initiate conversations with you and try to remind you of the good times the two of you had together. Remember, this is his tactic to gain control over you. You need to stay strong in such instances and remind yourself of your strengths, talents and potentials.

Make a list of all your qualities, strengths and accomplishments and every time you feel low, go through the list. Create positive affirmations centered on those qualities such as 'I am confident', 'I am a great artist', 'I have great writing skills', 'I am loving and compassionate' and so on and chant them out loud to rewire your mind to think positively. This shifts your attention from the demeaning things your abuser said to you to positive thoughts and helps you stick to your goal.

You need to consistently work on these guidelines to yield positive, results over time. It will take the tactics some time to yield the desired results so stay strong and patient, and soon you will find your abuser acting normally with you. In addition, make sure you set clear, healthy boundaries with your abuser to make him/her treat you with respect. The following chapter will focus on setting boundaries.

Chapter 4:
Set Clear Boundaries and Follow Through with Them

Narcissists are self-absorbed and believe that they are entitled to do anything they want including snooping through your personal stuff, belittling you whenever they get the chance to, depriving you of care and even financial needs, taking away all your civil, financial and social rights, and even throwing things at you if they want.

This happens because you fail to set any boundaries in your relationship with them. Whether your abuser is your friend, relative, parent, colleague, spouse or child, you must set clear and healthy boundaries with them and follow through with the rules at all costs.

Only when your abuser knows he/she needs to act a certain way with you, and sees you taking measures to make him/her comply with the rules will he or she slowly change his/her behavior accordingly. This won't come easy to you particularly because you have always allowed them be in control, but to regain your sanity, you need to take control of your life and for that, setting boundaries is only crucial.

Identify the Boundaries You Want to Set

First, think of all the boundaries you want in your relationship with that narcissist. Think of your core values and principles, the type of relationship you want to have with him/her and how you wish to be treated and then define boundaries accordingly. For instance, there should be no name calling, snooping into your personal stuff, harsh and violent behavior and so on in the relationship.

Communicate the Boundaries

Once you are clear on the rules you want in that relationship, communicate your concerns with him/her. Sit him/her down for a cordial talk and tell him/her how you feel about your relationship with him/her. Let him/her know he/she will get his/her fair share of time to speak, but before that, he/she must patiently listen to you.

Communicate all the boundaries you have identified to him/her and let him/her know that from now onwards, you expect him/her to oblige to those rules. Ensure that you talk about the implications of not respecting the boundaries you have set. For instance, if he/she belittles you or insults you in front of people, tell him/her that you'll stop seeing him/her. In case, he/she sneaks into your personal bank account, you may move out of the apartment. He/she must be aware of what may happen in case he/she does not respect a boundary.

Follow Through with the Rule

Make sure that you follow through with the boundary and make him/her comply with that by enforcing the consequence in case he/she does not oblige to the request. If you told him/her you will not speak to him/her if he/she gaslights you or questions your sanity, stop speaking to him/her unless he/she reaches out to you and apologizes for his/her unacceptable behavior.

You need to ensure that you don't give idle threats to your abuser and follow through with them if you find him/her overstepping the boundaries. Do this a few times and he/she is likely comply the next time. For instance, if you have a colleague who parks his truck in a manner that makes it tough for you to reverse your car and back it out, begin by firmly asking him her to leave enough space for other cars and after two times, state the consequences for not obliging to the request. You can then have his/her car towed, or report the incident to the HR department, but you must do it so he/she knows you just don't talk the talk, but walk it too.

Stand Your Ground

When you stand up to your narcissistic abuser, he/she will react to your new and changed behavior. You may find him/her coming back to you with certain demands of his own and may also try to guilt trap you or label you as a control freak. At this point, just stand your ground and do not give in to any such accusations or his/her new demands.

Let him/her know that while you are not leaving him/her, you are not going to accept abusive and manipulative behavior at any cost and that the boundaries that you have set are only healthy and legitimate. If they cannot comply with the rules, that's not your fault and that they should only talk to you only when it is essential. You must not take a step backward at this point, or they will stop taking you seriously.

You need to stay strong and resolute during this time to ensure your efforts yield good results. Your abuser may retaliate, but you need to maintain your calm and not react to things he/she says or does. The next chapter teaches you how to do that so he/she stops pestering you and leaves you alone.

Chapter 5:
Keep Your Calm and Put an End to the Vicious Cycle of Abuse

It is difficult not to react to the annoying things narcissists do to get your attention and interfere with your life, but during such times, you need to maintain your cool and treat them silently. Once you stop reacting and start responding to their behavior, can you put a permanent end to their vicious cycle of abuse.

Do Not React to His/ Her Comments

When your abuser sees you acting strongly and giving him/her silent treatment, he/she may try to do things to upset you. He/she may show up at your workplace and throw a tantrum, or belittle you in front of your friends, or sell off your stuff without your permission, or even accuse you falsely. If this happens, excuse yourself from the situation, take deep breaths and maintain your calm.

Every time he/she pulls off a bizarre stunt, understand that they are doing so to get your attention. You must not do any of the following at this point:

- Apologize to him/her for behaving firmly as it will only make you come off as the weaker person and entitle him/her.

- Explain yourself to him/her and seek his/her understanding because that will only portray you as someone needy for his/her care and attention.

- Retaliate and do something hurtful to him/her such as demean him/her publicly. The more you try to pick a fight with him/her, the more you will trigger his/her abusive behavior and compel him/her to control you more.

- Praise him/her and be nice to him/her because this behavior will only expose your weakness to him/her.

Always excuse yourself from the situation when your abuser tries to get back at you and do not give in to your reactive thoughts.

Think Things Through

Spend some time alone and calm yourself down. When you feel better, think of the best way to respond to his/her behavior and come up with different ideas. If he/she created a huge scene at your workplace, first apologize to your boss for it and then speak to your abuser firmly. Also, follow through with the consequence you set to make him/her understand that you won't give in to his/her abusive behavior. Always think things through before making a decision so that you do what's right for you.

Do Not Fall Prey to His/ Her Verbal Trickery

Narcissists have a way with language and use it tactfully to make a way to your heart and then control your mind. You need to look out for the following verbal tricks and counteract them effectively to disarm him/her completely.

- If he/she blames you for anything he/she did, firmly tell him/her you are well aware of your behavior and know who is at fault. Do not give him/her a chance to carry on with the conversation and excuse yourself from the situation.
- If he/she abuses you or says something mean to you and covers it up with 'I was only joking' or 'You are too sensitive', firmly remind him/her of the boundaries you set in place and let them know that even if the suggestion was meant in good humor, you don't appreciate such jokes, and that he/she must cut back on them.
- If he/she tells you of how special his/her relationship is with you and uses this trick to make you surrender to his/her manipulative behavior, let him/her know that even though you like being with him/her, you won't comply with controlling behavior.
- If he/she tells you of how only you have a problem with him/her and everybody else seems fine with him/her, point out clear instances wherein he/she abused others.

In addition, never go to your abuser with your problems but get advice from genuinely caring people because seeking advice from a narcissist will only allow him to overpower you.

Build Your Support System

While you work on all of the above, look out for genuinely caring and supportive people to build your own support system so that you have a group of people who have your back. This helps you stay sane and committed to your goal.

Look out for some genuinely caring people in your social circle preferably those who have time and again told you that you are living with a narcissist and offered you help to tame him/her. Reach out to such people and talk to them about your feelings. If they genuinely care for you, they will make you feel heard and validated, and agree to help you without judging you. Ensure to meet at least one person from your support system every week to have a direct conversation with him/her and can discuss your stories, feelings and progress with him/her in detail.

If, however, there is no such person in your immediate social circle, join some helpful groups on social media and look out for people who are ready to support victims of narcissistic abuse. It is important to have someone to talk to on regular basis so start cultivating your support system now.

Spend Quality Time with Yourself

Ensure that you spend quality time with yourself daily looking after your needs and doing things that make you happy and bring you closer to achieving your goals. The more you care for yourself, the more you will feel in control of your life and the more you will appear unattractive to your narcissistic abuser. You can only think calmly and rationally if you feel peaceful from within and that peace does not come unless and until you feel validated and happy.

You cannot always rely on people to make you feel acknowledged. You need to be the first person to do that yourself and this begins with you taking out time for your own needs. Every day, spend at least an hour engaging in a fun activity, a hobby you love or anything that relaxes you. Mondays can be library days when you visit your local library and pick a good book for the week. Tuesdays can be massage days when you treat yourself to a relaxing, full body massage. Thursdays can be painting days when you paint your heart out and so on. If taking out an hour in a single go is difficult, have 2 to 3 relaxing sessions of 30 or 20 minutes each, respectively. The idea is to simply make you do something nice for yourself so that you feel loved and cared for.

When you spend quality time with yourself regularly, you feel good and happy about yourself and stop seeking care and love from your narcissistic abuser. In addition, when you feel good from within, it only becomes easier to ignore your abuser and move on happily with your life.

Understand the Abusive Cycle and Curb it

You may deny this, but living with a narcissist does make you somewhat immune to the abuse and even crave for a volatile episode after some time. You and your abuser share a codependent relationship of sorts wherein you are his/her care provider and he/she is the care receiver. Even though you are in charge of providing him/her with care and affection, you enjoy being in that position even with all the hurt and pain it brings with itself.

When a certain period of time passes by and you haven't had a hard time with your abuser, you may do something to trigger his/her mood swings in hopes of bringing back some excitement in your life. You miss out on the excitement and the closeness you share once the volatile phase ends so you do something to upset him/her. When you do threaten him/her to leave, he/she comes running back to you and showers you with affection and apologies giving you what you were looking for in the first place. Both of you feel happy for a while and this cycle continues for good.

This is a vicious cycle and you may not realize it, but it is only confusing and upsetting you more not to mention making your abuser more powerful with time. If you wish to stop being attractive to your abuser, you need to put an end to this cycle by doing the following:

- If it has been quite a while since your abuser contacted you, or did something to hurt you, or has been giving you silent treatment, let it be that way and do not approach him/her yourself.

- Be aware of your feelings and thoughts and how they make you behave. If you find yourself thinking about your abuser a lot and feel tempted to talk to him/her or do something that may bring him/her closer to you and initiate the abusive cycle, acknowledge that feeling instead of shunning it. When you accept your feelings, they stop rattling inside you, which makes it easier for you to address them.

- Understand that you yearn for someone's love and attention, and remind yourself of what happens when you give power to your abuser. Spend some time with a loving friend and look for new people to build healthier relationships with.

- Make sure not to talk to or meet your abuser until the time you have your temptation under control and do not react to it. Engage in calming and fun activities during this time, and if it helps, block your abuser for a while on your phone and social media if you do not live with him/her.

- Once a considerable period of time has passed and you no longer feel the need to engage with him/her, it is safe to meet him/her now.

- During that time, if you do meet him/her, do not share your stories of feeling withdrawn, lonely or missing out on him/her because the minute you portray your vulnerability to your abuser, you appear attractive to him/her. You need to act strong and resolute so he/she does not feel drawn to you and if you keep doing that, he/she will stop abusing and controlling you.

While working on these guidelines, you may stumble and make a few slip—ups. You may give in to your urge to contact him/her or may not stick to the plan as desired. In such times, be kind to yourself, engage in positive self-talk and get back up to start afresh every time. You do that constantly and there will come a time when you will overpower your abuser completely.

Conclusion

We have come to the end of the book. Thank you for reading and congratulations for reading until the end.

I hope this book provided you with the value you were looking for. Use the information in this book to overcome narcissistic abuse.

If you found the book valuable, can you recommend it to others? One way to do that is to post a review on Amazon.

Click here to leave a review for this book on Amazon!

Thank you and good luck!